RISKY BUSINESS

Stunt Woman

Daredevil Specialist

By

KEITH ELLIOT GREENBERG

Photographs by Tom Sanders

A BLACKBIRCH PRESS BOOK

WOODBRIDGE, CONNECTICUT

Published by Blackbirch Press, Inc.
260 Amity Road
Woodbridge, CT 06525

©1997 Blackbirch Press, Inc.
All photos ©Tom Sanders/Aerial Focus, except page 20,
photo by Mike Allen.
First Edition

Printed and manufactured in the United States

10 9 8 7 6 5 4 3 2 1

Library of Congress Cataloging-in-Publication Data

Greenberg, Keith Elliot.
    Stunt woman/by Keith Elliot Greenberg.—1st ed.
        p.   cm. — (Risky business)
    Includes bibliographical references and index.
    Summary: Profiles the life of professional stunt woman Jan
Davis.
    ISBN 1-56711-159-9 (alk. paper)
    1. Davis, Jan (Jan Marie)—Juvenile literature. 2. Women
stunt performers—United States—Biography—Juvenile
literature. 3. Stunt performers—United States—Biography—
Juvenile literature. [1. Davis, Jan (Jan Marie). 2. Stunt
performers. 3. Women—Biography.] I. Title. II. Series: Risky
business (Woodbridge, Conn.)
PN1998.3.D382G74   1997
791.43'028'092—dc20
[B]   95-38737
                                                                                       CIP

ODUCTION

Jan Davis's friends sometimes worry about her. And they have good reason. After all, her job does involve para-chuting into trees and onto buildings, jumping off water-falls and radio towers, and walking on the wings of air-planes! As a professional stunt woman, however, Jan won't allow fear to get the better of her. Too much worrying, she argues, only stops a person from living out their dreams.

"I have one friend who's always warning me to be careful," she says. "Then, one day, my friend tore a kneecap—just stepping out of a car. That never happened to me, and I jump out of planes for a living."

3

When a character in a movie, television show, or commercial is seen doing physically demanding stunts, a person like Jan is often the one who is actually doing the action. With her long, flowing blonde hair, Jan sometimes substitutes for the production's leading lady, but she also does scenes for male stars.

What kind of person gets involved in this kind of risky business? "You have to be a thrill-seeker, I guess," Jan admits with a smile.

As a stunt woman, Jan does the action that is too dangerous for actors to do.

4

Jan has had a bold spirit of adventure since her childhood.

Jan learned how to be adventurous from her father, Dave Smith. While Jan and her mother, Marcy, were home in Santa Barbara, California, Dave was traveling to exotic places in search of riches. He discovered a fortune in the Central American country of Honduras, where he opened a gold mine.

Then, when Jan was in high school, tragedy struck. Her father was flying a plane filled with TNT, to blast a

hole into a mountain that he believed contained gold. There was no airport near the gold mine, so Dave tried to land in a cow pasture. He circled over the field first, to scare the cows away. But, just as he was about to land, one of the animals stepped in front of the craft. The plane crashed into the cow, and the explosives on board blew up. Jan's father was killed immediately.

Jan's career requires that she be in top physical condition.

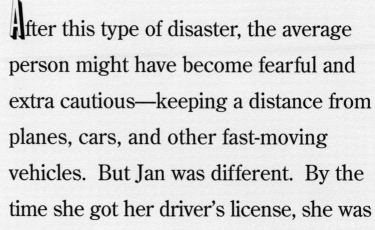

After this type of disaster, the average person might have become fearful and extra cautious—keeping a distance from planes, cars, and other fast-moving vehicles. But Jan was different. By the time she got her driver's license, she was competing for trophies at auto races.

At the time, there were no categories for female racers, so Jan competed against the males. "I was always a little bit of a tomboy," she remembers. "What I really loved was going fast and beating the guys."

At age 20, Jan bought herself a Porsche sports car and was soon making a name

As a longtime thrill-seeker, Jan has also tackled auto racing and downhill skiing.

for herself in auto racing. For two straight years, she was Women's West Coast Champion.

Jan then became interested in skiing, after she suffered the death of another loved one. Her first husband died by mixing his blood pressure medication with cold pills—never realizing that the combination was deadly.

9

The terrible loss caused Jan to become even more obsessed with danger and sport. "The only time I could be comfortable with myself was when I was racing down a difficult hill," Jan says. "I was so caught up in grief, that was my way of escaping."

Jan looked for the most challenging places to ski. "I'd go to the highest point of a mountain and wait until a more experienced skier went down the hard-est slope," she explains. "Then, I'd just fall in behind, and follow whatever that person was doing."

When she's not skydiving, Jan will often go scuba diving for fun.

11

Jan enjoys learning many skills, including how to use a camera.

Not surprisingly, Jan wasn't happy simply diving out of an airplane and parachuting to the ground. She wanted to master every new sport. To help her, she hired Tom Sanders—a professional cameraman who was also a skydiver—to film her jumps. Tom and Jan would view the footage and discuss her mistakes. In time, Tom also taught Jan how to operate a camera. Eventually, the couple married.

"Like everything else, I pushed skydiving to the limit," Jan says proudly.

Jan and Tom prepare for a dive together.

In 1988, Jan was a member of the Olympic skydiving team at the Olympic Games in Seoul, Korea. She also helped a group of other skydivers—clad in colorful outfits—organize a formation of the Olympic rings in the sky, as Tom filmed them.

13

Once, Tom was given an assignment to film a group of men parachuting off Autana, a 4,000-foot cliff in a remote section of Venezuela's jungle. Jan came along to help. This type of dive is known as a "base jump"—rather than jumping out of a plane, the person falls from a fixed object such as a building, bridge, or mountain. Jan had never base jumped before, but she was fascinated.

"I hung over the edge of the cliff, and filmed the men going off," she says. "Then, when the last of them had jumped, I went over to the edge and jumped, too."

"I became the fifth person to ever jump off that cliff," Jan boasts. "And to this day, nobody else has done it."

High in the air, Jan enjoys a freedom that few have experienced.

Jan in freefall, during her historic jump at Angel Falls.

In 1988, Jan received international attention by becoming the first woman to jump off Venezuela's Angel Falls. This massive waterfall is the tallest in the world, measuring 3,212 feet— three times the height of the Empire State Building!

"To me, it wasn't a big deal to be the first woman," she says. "Just to jump it was a thrill."

17

"When you jump out of an airplane, you jump out the door onto a cushion of air created by the movement of the plane," Jan explains. "It's like when you're in a car and you stick your hand out the window—your hand just rolls around in the wind.

"But when you jump off a fixed object, you start off at zero speed. So there's the feeling of falling. During the first five seconds, you build up speed, and the cushion of air builds up under your body. Soon, you begin to fly. At Angel Falls, I could clearly see rock and the waterfall going by me, and the jungle floor coming up. It was incredibly beautiful."

As a cushion of air builds up under a skydiver's body, it creates the feeling of flying.

Pictures of Jan diving off Angel Falls ended up in magazines all over the world. Tom sold film footage of the event to numerous TV shows. News programs started doing stories on this unique husband-and-wife team. Their leap off a 1,600-foot radio antenna in Maine was featured on an ABC television network special.

Jan's favorite pastime had quickly become her career. Her telephone was now ringing with offers to perform stunts in various productions.

Tom and Jan fly through the air together.

Jan jumps from
a radio antenna
in Maine for a
television special.

Jan (mouse) and
Tom (bear) sky-
dive in costume.

During one stunt, Jan flies over to Brutus the skydiving dog and his owner Ron Sirull.

She appeared in the television program "Civil Wars," pretending to be actress Mariel Hemingway. "Her character was going to jump from a plane to get her boyfriend's attention," Jan laughs. "Except, when you watched the show, it was really me skydiving."

In singer Paul Simon's music video "Thelma," male and female puppets are seen dancing together before diving through the air. "I was dressed up as one of the puppets, and I did a skydive," Jan points out. "I didn't realize I was playing a puppet until I saw the video."

23

Jan and Brad Hood prepare for a shot during the filming of "Puppet Masters."

After doing stunts for *Point Break* with Patrick Swayze and Keanu Reeves, Jan played a man in the science fiction film, *Puppet Masters.* She was supposed to be an army commando sent to dive from a plane onto a building at night, in search of an alien breeding ground.

In January 1995, Jan began work on *Congo*, an adventure movie filmed in the Central American jungle of Costa Rica. This is home to the largest-known population of bushmasters, the world's deadliest snakes. As Jan says, "They call them 'two-step snakes' because, after they bite you, you take two steps, then drop dead. They live in trees—next to the hornet's nests—and, of course, I was skydiving and landing in those trees."

Jan in costume during the filming of "Congo."

Wing-walking high above California.

"The danger with a tree landing is that it's easy to fall through the tree onto the ground. So you smack into the tree hard enough for your parachute to get tangled in the branches. Once the scene is over, you hang there until a helicopter comes and rescues you."

When she isn't skydiving, Jan is scuba diving or walking around on the wings of airplanes. While some stunt people get on the wing and stand still as the plane does a maneuver, Jan moves around. She also does a routine in which she lowers the ladder from the bottom of the craft and climbs on it. Only when the plane turns upside down does she take a special precaution: strapping herself to a pole on the wing.

To be prepared, Jan works out with weights. "You have to be strong for wing-walking," she says. "You're climbing around on a plane going 100 miles-per-hour. Sometimes you have to grab onto the wing, and boost yourself up."

From time to time, Jan has injured herself during practice. But she's never gotten hurt on a stunt assignment. "When I'm practicing, I'm finding out what my limits are," she explains. "By the time I'm on the job, I know them."

 Jan loves to do stunts that challenge her skills.

**Much of Jan's time off
is spent practicing
new techniques
and stunts.**

On a day off, Jan and Tom call a friend with a plane and arrange for Jan to practice some new tricks in the sky over the Santa Barbara beach. Jan often doesn't wear a parachute during these sessions because she's worried about it opening accidently and getting caught in the rudder. But she does one stunt where she pretends to fall off the wing, then pulls the parachute as onlookers scream in horror.

For Jan, the risks
she takes are
simply a part
of daily life.

"I guess you can say that you can't really enjoy your life until you overcome your fear," Jan says thoughtfully. "When you live in fear, you spend your life being afraid of things that may never happen."

Then she smiles and adds, "I don't live like that."

31

FURTHER READING

Cherrell, Gwen. *How Movies Are Made*. New York: Facts On File, 1989.

Gibbons, Gail. *Lights! Camera! Action!: How a Movie Is Made*. New York: HarperCollins Children's Books, 1985.

Limousin, Odile, and Neumann, Daniele. *TV and Films: Behind the Scenes*. Lake Forest, IL: Forest House Publishing, 1993.

Nentl, Jerolyn. *Skydiving*. New York: Macmillan Children's Book Group, 1978.

Scott, Elaine. *Movie Magic: Behind the Scenes with Special Effects*. New York: Morrow, 1995.

INDEX